Endorsements for *A Practical Guide to Crofting Law*

"An invaluable practical guide to demystify crofting law and to help crofters, potential crofters and crofting communities understand their rights and obligations as crofters and members of those communities – highly recommended."

- Sir Crispin Agnew of Lochnaw Bt QC, Chairman, Crofting Law Group and Author of 'Crofting Law' (2000)

"The law relating to crofting in the Highlands and Islands of Scotland is notoriously complex. Brian is one person who knows his way around it. His guidance will be found beneficial to those new to the subject and those with specific matters in mind. Whilst changes are afoot, his take on the current state of play will be invaluable to lawyers and lay persons alike."

- Derek Flyn, Co-Author of 'Crofting Law' (1990), 'Crofting Law Sump Report' (2014) and 'Crofting Law' (2017); former Chair of the Scottish Crofting Federation; and Crofting Law Consultant, Inksters Solicitors

"This is an extremely helpful guide to crofting law which will help all who have to navigate the Byzantine routes through the law of the land."

- Tavish Scott, Member of the Scottish Parliament for Shetland and Co-Convener, Scottish Parliament Cross-Party Group on Crofting

"Lawyers will hate this book – it takes a complex subject and makes it understandable to the layman. The level of detail is sufficient for understanding without getting bogged down in jargon."

- Russell Smith, Crofter and former Chair, Scottish Crofting Federation

"This is a book that has been awaited since crofting law was formed, a book that lays out what the, notoriously difficult to navigate, "sea of legislation" is about. The ambition of writing a ***practical*** *guide to crofting law has been achieved by Scotland's leading* ***practising*** *crofting lawyer.*

As well as providing a service to clients and advice to government and other organisations, Brian Inkster delivers a session on crofting law on the Scottish Crofting Federation's training programme. Feedback from students credits him with opening their eyes to how fascinating crofting law actually is.

Brian is a natural storyteller (it comes in the Shetland genes perhaps) and he has written this book as a travel writer would introduce us to exotic parts – setting the scene with the history and background, the introduction of the inhabitants and roles they play; the unique culture of crofting and the many unsuspected twists. It gives all the essential information needed to sail that "sea of legislation" and to safely visit the many crofting islands therein. It will be the essential reading for crofting students and for all who want to navigate crofting law."

- Patrick Krause, Chief Executive, Scottish Crofting Federation

"An accessible overview of a complex legal specialism which would be a useful addition to the shelf of anyone involved in crofting."

- Katy Dickson, Head of Policy, Scottish Land & Estates

"Brian Inkster is to be congratulated on unravelling the complexities of crofting law into a practical guide that is comprehensive and yet can be easily understood. I am sure this will prove to be a very useful guide to current crofters and those with an interest in crofting."

- Andrew McCornick, President, NFU Scotland

"Brian has produced what I regard to be an easily digested and readable guide which can be of immense help to those seeking to steer their way through what at times can be a daunting maze called crofting law.

His unquestionable grasp of crofting legislation shines through in what he has written for the benefit of others."

- Iain M Maciver, Factor, Stornoway Trust; Commissioner, Crofting Commission; and Vice-Chairman, Crofting Law Group

"Usually when I pick up a book aiming to understand law I lose interest within a few pages due to the complexity of legal jargon used by the author. Not so Brian Inkster's first foray to print. His debut book, which like himself is dynamic in nature, provides an insightful summarisation of crofting law, which is easy to follow yet reasonably comprehensive in its detail. It touches on all the popular themes relating to crofting regulation of the modern day and will, I am sure, quickly become an essential for the crofter's bookshelf."

- David Campbell, Rural Surveyor and Commissioner, Crofting Commission

"Congratulations to Brian Inkster on producing a completely straight-forward guide to a subject which is pretty much the exact opposite of straightforward; a point beautifully illustrated by the list of relevant legislation. Brian lists a total of 17 separate pieces of legislation affecting crofters/crofting which have been introduced in the 24 years since 1995, yet according to the Crofting Commission's Annual Report there appeared in 2017/18 to be just over 20,000 crofts. Never in the history of Scotland – indeed in the history of the United Kingdom – can so much legislation have been passed to regulate so few!

A Practical Guide to Crofting Law provides a very comprehensive yet readable work to a very complicated subject. It is a guide that should make it much easier for (non-expert) parties concerned with crofting to live together."

- John Mackenzie, Crofting Landlord, owner of Gairloch and Conon Estates

"I knew as soon as I glanced at this piece of work by Brian Inkster, that it would be really useful. As a former Chair of the Crofters Commission, a lifelong crofter, and somebody still engaged in the increasingly labyrinthine toils of the crofting regulatory system, I am well acquainted with the various Crofting Acts, including the rather shambolic 2010 version, and with a number of much longer books on crofting legislation. This, much more concise, and doing what it says on the tin is not a replacement for the others, but it is a very valuable addition to the toolkit.

Quite short, the book is very well laid out and clear, and as someone who has known Brian for a long time, I can hear his voice coming through clearly. The heads are exactly as I would have hoped they would be, and it is very easy for me to move to the specific issue upon which I require clarity. Having speed read the whole book (a tribute to its clarity), I can say that the only bit not relevant to my purposes is the section on the community right to buy. And that is only because nobody in Shetland has ever evinced even a momentary interest in that particular option."

- Drew Ratter, Crofter and former Chair, Crofters Commission

"This is a useful and accessible addition to the available texts on this complex area of law. It will provide an initial or more general understanding which I am sure may prove helpful to many."

- Bruce Beveridge, former President, Law Society of Scotland

"Brian's book represents a significant and, most importantly, accurate introduction to crofting law. Whether you're someone looking to buy a croft and don't know what one is or you're from a crofting background and have grown up around crofting and the legislative quirks, I am certain that you will find something new and interesting in this fantastic publication.

The struggle for the rights of Crofters has not been and never was simple. By introducing the reader to the human element of crofting at the beginning, Brian has given an authentic and meaningful tone to the whole book.

This book will be an invaluable resource for Young Crofters and new entrants starting out in the industry. Understanding crofting legislation is not straight forward and this book will be a go to resource in years to come."

- Donald MacKinnon, Crofter and Vice-Chair, Scottish Crofting Federation

"I found the book to be an admirably accessible and well-structured guide to the basics of crofting law, a notoriously Byzantine field, and would recommend it as a quick reference guide to this apparently daunting subject."

- Brendan O'Hanrahan, Vice-Chair, Scottish Crofting Federation

"Crofting Law is a fact, despite this it is at times ignored, at times misunderstood by relevant professions. This is an unworthy indictment.

Brian Inkster's book is a very welcome explanation of a legal statute which must remain fit for purpose for those communities it was designed to protect."

- Ronnie Eunson, Crofter/Farmer; Director, Quality Meat Scotland; Chair, Scottish Islands Abattoirs Association; former Commissioner, Crofters Commission; and former Chair, Shetland Livestock Marketing Group

"Easy to read and digest, Brian's book on the basics of crofting law will no doubt provide a useful quick reference source not just for solicitors, but for crofters and landlords too. It covers all the key points and simplifies for the reader this complex area of law."

- Martin Minton, Crofting Solicitor, Inksters Solicitors

"Crofting law can sometimes seem like an existential exercise, wondering how to make sense of a confusing set of rules in an uncertain world. It is not possible to discuss crofting without reference to the law, and as the book shows, there is a considerable body of legislation which underpins the subject. Because it is a practical guide, the book does not seek to analyse this complex legislative regime. What it offers is an introduction to crofting law for anyone who is interested in the subject, does not already have a strong grasp of the subject, and wants to understand the layout of the ground in front of them.

Each chapter concerns a key topic necessary to understanding crofting law. The purpose of each chapter is to explain that topic by a discussion of the main points a person with little or no knowledge of the subject needs to have in order to understand it. There are frequent references to other sources of useful information, which is a very useful aspect of the book.

Crofts can be in the form of tenanted land, owner-occupied land, or deemed crofts. The text points out that identifying tenanted land as a croft can be complex, but highlights the practical significance of the effect of a croft having been entered onto the Register of Crofts. It also provides a helpful definition of what constitutes an owner-occupied croft. Other topics covered by the book include buying a croft (whether it is tenanted or owner-occupied), removing croft land from crofting regulation, sub-leasing a croft, and transferring the owner or tenant's interest in a croft following the death of a crofter.

This book is a useful introduction to a notoriously difficult and specialised area of law. It is written in a clear and understandable style. The author is a very well-known lawyer who has dedicated many years of practice to the subject. He has brought that experience to this book, distilling down the many intricacies of the law to its "real world" essentials. For those wanting to understand how crofting works, this book provides them with what they need to know."

- Robert Sutherland, Advocate, MCIArb

"A Practical Guide to Crofting Law by Brian Inkster provides an easy-to-follow overview of crofting law, its history and its complexities.

This will be an essential tool for those contemplating the acquisition of a croft, those new to crofting, or indeed any existing crofter considering altering the administrative status quo of his or her holding and seeking guidance.

Whether assignation, succession, resumption, sublet, development, purchase of a tenanted croft from its landowner, or any other of the many processes required by statute, this book will guide you through the intricate web of legislation.

Equally practical for landowners, agents, advisers and anyone interested in the subject, this layman's handbook will be a frequently-read resource.

Explanations of the working of the Scottish Land Court and the Crofting Commission, and reference to crofters' representative organisation the Scottish Crofting Foundation, fill in the vital background detail of crofting. A brief overview of the grants system for crofters is an added bonus, as are pointers on how to find a croft to take on, and the various ways that can be done.

When I was crofting adviser for the Scottish Crofters Union back in the late eighties and the nineties, my copy of Flyn and MacCuish's Crofting Law was a well-thumbed source which enabled me to help our members with some of the myriad issues which challenge crofters and crofting representatives alike.

Brian Inkster's work will fulfil the same role, and when used in conjunction with Flyn and Graham's 2017 book Crofting Law, and reference to the findings of the Scottish Land Court, will provide chapter and verse on crofting legalities."

- Fiona Mandeville, Crofter; former employee, Scottish Crofters Union; former Chair, Scottish Crofting Federation; and editor of the Scottish Crofting Federation's publication 'The Crofter'

A Practical Guide to Crofting Law

A Practical Guide to Crofting Law

Brian Inkster
LLB, Dip LP
Solicitor, Inksters

Law Brief Publishing

Published 2019 by Law Brief Publishing, an imprint of Law Brief Publishing Ltd
30 The Parks
Minehead
Somerset
TA24 8BT

www.lawbriefpublishing.com

Paperback: 978-1-912687-39-8

Dedicated to:-

My wife Nicola Walls

for her forbearance, love and support

and to:-

My parents Lol and Doris Inkster

for their advice when I set out on my own in the world to "do whatever you think best dear". I am sorry that they never lived long enough to see this book published and other such 'best' things.

ABOUT THE AUTHOR

Brian Inkster is a solicitor specialising in crofting law.

He is the Hon Secretary of the Crofting Law Group, a member of the Crofting Group of Scottish Land & Estates, the Cross-Party Group on Crofting at the Scottish Parliament, the Scottish Government Crofting Stakeholder Forum, the Crofting Register Stakeholder Forum and the Scottish Government Crofting Bill Group.

Brian blogs about crofting law at the Crofting Law Blog (croftinglawblog.com) and regularly writes articles for The Crofter (the trade magazine of the Scottish Crofting Federation). He also provides comment and articles to local and national newspapers and magazines such as The West Highland Free Press, The Shetland Times, The Oban Times, The Northern Times, The Scotsman, The Herald, The Press & Journal, The Scottish Farmer, Scottish Legal News and The Journal of the Law Society of Scotland.

Brian also gives talks on crofting law to universities and at conferences, workshops and seminars. He has provided detailed submissions to the Scottish Government on proposed crofting law reform.

Brian has been interviewed about crofting law on BBC Alba, BBC Reporting Scotland and Sunday Politics Scotland. He has also been interviewed about crofting law on local and national Scottish radio news programmes.

Brian was born and brought up in Shetland. He is the son of a fisherman rather than a crofter. He studied law at the University of Edinburgh before moving to Glasgow in 1991 to undertake his legal traineeship. Following conclusion of his traineeship Brian continued to practice law in Glasgow where he founded his own law firm, Inksters, in 1999. Inksters now also have offices in Aberdeen, Edinburgh, Forfar, Inverness, Lerwick, Portree, Thurso and Wick.

Inksters provide a free legal advice helpline on crofting law to members of the Scottish Crofting Federation. Brian provides tutoring on Acquiring and Evaluating a Croft / Crofting Law Basics to the Access to Crofting Toolkit Course run by the Scottish Crofting Federation.

Brian has been involved in a number of significant reported decisions of the Scottish Land Court: Marquis of Zetland v Johnson 2004 SLCR 171, Reference by Crofters Commission under Sec 53 Crofters (Scotland) Act 1993 2012 SLCR 159, Rodenhurst v Thrumster Estate Ltd (No 1) 2015 SLCR 14, Rodenhurst v Thrumster Estate Ltd (No 2) 2015 SLCR 26, Grains v Gifford's Executors & Others 2016 SLCR 86, Kennedy v Smith 2016 SLCR 94 and Thrumster Estate Ltd v Mindt 2016 SLCR 144.

Brian also has a speciality in the law of servitudes (easements) having acted for the pursuers in Moncrieff v Jamieson. This case was ultimately decided in the House of Lords and has been described by Professor Roddy Paisley as "one of the most important cases on servitudes in the last 100 years". It established for the first time in law that, in certain circumstances, you can have a servitude right to park a car ancillary to a right of access.

Brian obtained the distinction of being named Solicitor of the Year at the Law Awards of Scotland in 2006. He was called "a one man Scottish legal institution" in the Recommended Law Firm Guide 2010. At the Law Awards of Scotland in 2014 he was recognised as Managing Partner of the Year.

Brian has an active interest in entrepreneurship, marketing, technology and corporate social responsibility in relation to running a law firm. He is often asked to speak on these topics at conferences, summits and retreats.

Mitch Kowalski in his book, 'The Great Legal Reformation: Notes from the Field', wrote:-

> *"Brian Inkster reminds me of what Elvis Costello would look like if he had become a lawyer: Inkster has an understated, new-wave coolness about him that fits nicely with his role as a legal entrepreneur—and he does kind of look like Elvis Costello in his prime. Kind of."*

PREFACE

A croft has been described as *"an area of land surrounded by a sea of legislation"*.

When the Rural Affairs, Climate Change and Environment Committee of the Scottish Parliament were taking evidence in 2015 on the Scottish Government's amendments to the crofting community right to buy at Stage 2 of the Community Empowerment (Scotland) Bill this description was elaborated on by some of the participants.

When introducing themselves, at the outset, the late Alex Fergusson said:-

> *"I am the MSP for Galloway and West Dumfries, and crofting law is a complete mystery to me."*

Then, after some discussion on the definition of crofting community, Alex Fergusson said:-

> *"That is me. I am exhausted."*

Earlier in the proceedings Peter Peacock of Community Land Scotland observed:-

> *"It is said that only three people understand crofting law—one is mad, one is dead and nobody can remember who the third one is."*

The aim of this book is to do what it says on the tin: To be a **practical guide** to crofting law. In the process I hope to demystify crofting law for those who struggle to understand it.

It is not a substitute for a detailed analysis of crofting law as given most recently by Derek Flyn and Keith Graham in 'Crofting Law' (2017), before that by Sir Crispin Agnew QC in 'Crofting Law' (2000) and in the beginning by Donald MacCuish and Derek Flyn in 'Crofting Law' (1990).

I won't give you footnote references to, or tables of, statutes, orders, rules, regulations or cases.

It is an introduction to crofting law for those with an interest in it or who may touch upon it. Whether that is lawyers, law students, land agents, crofters, landlords, Members of the Scottish Parliament or anyone else with an interest in it.

I will cover the main issues briefly and concisely. This will hopefully highlight the complexity of crofting law and the pitfalls and traps that await the uninitiated. The aim is that you will, as a result, be better versed in the basics of crofting law (and may well find the answers that you seek in these pages) but may have to delve deeper or seek assistance for more complex matters.

I would like to thank Tim Kevan and Garry Wright of Law Brief Publishing for encouraging me to write this book and, of course, for publishing it.

I also thank Donna Smith, for clarifying some specific points for me, and Martin Minton, Ronnie Eunson, Tavish Scott, Katy Dickson, Lucy Sumsion, John Mackenzie, Jim McPherson and Brendan O'Hanrahan for making useful comments and suggested amendments to my edited proof copy, many of which I incorporated into the final manuscript that you now have before you.

My wife, Nicola Walls, has put up with me being 'absent' when writing it including a 'holiday' week that she could not enjoy with me. For her forbearance, love and support I am eternally grateful.

The law is stated as at 1 March 2019.

Brian Inkster
March 2019

CONTENTS

CHAPTER ONE
CROFTING LAW HISTORY AND LEGISLATION

Highland Clearances and the Crofters' War

Crofting Law came about as a result of the Highland Clearances that were carried out during the 1800s. Landowners cleared tenants from their land, to make way for large scale sheep farms and deer forests, sometimes with a barbarity that left people homeless and was known to result in the death of the young or infirm shortly on the back thereof.

Often these displaced tenants emigrated from Scotland for a new life in Canada, the USA or Australia.

The unrest arising therefrom became known as the 'Crofters' War' of the 1870s and 1880s.

In 1874 an attempt to remove Bernera crofters from grazing land on the Isle of Lewis to inferior land on the Island of Great Bernera was met by successful resistance and the acquittal of three crofters charged with assault against a sheriff officer.

From 1879 to 1882 there was unrest in Lochbroom in Wester Ross where the eviction of crofters resulted in media support and it being reported that Highlanders resident in London had expressed their deepest sympathy with this oppression.

The culmination of the Crofters' War was undoubtedly an incident at Braes on the Isle of Skye in 1882. Crofters were refusing to pay rents due to the loss of common grazing land. A sheriff officer sent to serve eviction notices for non-payment of the rent was surrounded by the crofters who put the papers on a heap and set fire to them. By doing so the crofters committed the crime of deforcement. Fifty policemen were despatched from Glasgow to arrest the perpetrators. The crofters resisted with sticks and stones in what became known as the 'Battle of the Braes'.

There were also altercations between police and crofters at Glendale on the Isle of Skye resulting in a gunboat being despatched with a civil servant on board whose task was to try to persuade Glendale men to submit to the authority of the law. Four did so, were found guilty and given jail sentences of two months in Edinburgh in March 1883. But on being released from jail they returned to their crofting township in triumph as the 'Glendale Martyrs'.

The Napier Commission

As a result of these and other similar incidents of unrest the UK government initiated the Napier Commission *"to inquire into the conditions of the Crofters and Cottars in the Highlands and Islands of Scotland and all matters affecting the same or relating thereto"*. The first hearing of this Royal Commission into crofters' grievances took place at Ollach Schoolhouse at Braes on 8 May 1883.

From then until 26 December 1883 the Commission travelled extensively around the Highlands and Islands of Scotland holding 69 days of public hearings in some of the remotest parts of the country including even visits to the islands of St Kilda and Foula. They questioned 775 people, asking 46,750 questions in total.

Crofting Legislation

The inquiry led to the passing of the Crofters Holdings (Scotland) Act 1886 which gave crofters security of tenure, the right to a fair rent (with reviews every seven years) and the right to claim compensation for permanent improvements.

Various Acts of Parliament followed with perhaps the most significant being the Crofting Reform (Scotland) Act 1976 which gave crofters an absolute right to purchase their croft house and garden ground and the ability (but one that in certain circumstances can be blocked by a landlord) to purchase their croft.

In 1993 all existing crofting legislation was brought together (consolidated) into one piece of legislation: the Crofters (Scotland) Act 1993 ("the 1993 Act").

Following on from that consolidating Act there has been further legislation affecting crofting:-

- Transfer of Crofting Estates (Scotland) Act 1997 ("the 1997 Act")
- Land Reform (Scotland) Act 2003 ("the 2003 Act")
- Crofting Reform etc. Act 2007 ("the 2007 Act")
- Crofting Reform (Scotland) Act 2010 ("the 2010 Act")
- Crofting (Amendment) (Scotland) Act 2013 ("the 2013 Act")

- Community Empowerment (Scotland) Act 2015 ("the 2015 Act")
- Land Reform (Scotland) Act 2016 ("the 2016 Act")

There has also been minor or consequential amendments made to the 1993 Act by the following legislation:-

- Requirements of Writing (Scotland) Act 1995
- Planning (Consequential Provisions) (Scotland) Act 1997
- The Scotland Act 1998 (Consequential Modifications) (No.2) Order 1999
- Abolition of Feudal Tenure etc. (Scotland) Act 2000
- Agricultural Holdings (Scotland) Act 2003
- Title Conditions (Scotland) Act 2003
- Civil Partnership Act 2004
- The Civil Partnership Act 2004 (Consequential Amendments) (Scotland) Order 2005
- Housing (Scotland) Act 2014
- Bankruptcy (Scotland) Act 2016

Future Legislative Reform

Problems arose from the drafting of the 2010 Act that led to the apparent need for the 2013 Act (to allow owner-occupier crofters to decroft land). As a result of this it became clear to the Scottish Government that there were other problems in the existing legislation causing difficulties for crofters, landlords and others.

The Scottish Government gave a commitment to deal with those issues. The Crofting Law Group offered to assist in identifying the issues.

'One Scotland: the Government's Programme for Scotland 2014-15' states:-

> *"The Crofting Law Group will present a review of crofting legislation to the Scottish Government by the end of 2014, which will inform changes to both the legislation and administration of crofting that will be taken forward in early course. The Scottish Government will fully engage with the Crofting Law Group and wider stakeholder organisations to ensure buy-in to the changes."*

The Crofting Law Group arranged for the preparation of the 'Crofting Law Sump Report' by Derek Flyn and Keith Graham to collate and prioritise the issues and problems involved. That was presented to the Scottish Government in November 2014 with indications as to how the 57 issues/problems identified in the Report might be solved.

In their 2016 Manifesto the Scottish National Party (SNP) stated:-

> *"Crofters have long been concerned at overly complicated and outdated legislation so we will modernise crofting law and make it more transparent, understandable and workable in practice."*

Having formed the new minority Scottish Government in 2016 the SNP put in place a Crofting Bill Team to fulfil their Manifesto pledge. The Bill Team carried out consultations surrounding the legislative change sought and data from those consultations was analysed and a report produced in early 2018 by an independent third party for consideration by Scottish Ministers.

Following on from that report Fergus Ewing MSP, Cabinet Secretary for the Rural Economy with responsibility for crofting, announced a two-phase approach to crofting law reform.

During the current Scottish Parliamentary term (i.e. before 6 May 2021) it is likely that a Bill will be introduced to fix many of the more straightforward problems identified in the 'Crofting Law Sump Report'.

The second phase is longer term work, where Mr Ewing has asked his officials to continue with fundamentally reviewing crofting legislation to provide a solution to some of the more complex and challenging issues facing crofting, and what that might mean for how legislation is developed in future. This work has already begun but will be for a future Parliament to deliver.

CHAPTER TWO
CROFTS AND CROFTERS

What constitutes a croft in law is a complex set of rules going back to 1886 that can be quite difficult to fathom out. This makes the simple definition set out in the Preface to this book of a croft being *"an area of land surrounded by a sea of legislation"* a very apt one.

For present purposes, and on the whole, you can simply rely on the fact that a holding is a croft if it has been registered in the Register of Crofts (Chapter 5). This is especially so following the 2007 Act which introduced a prescriptive period of 20 years for constituting a croft if it had been so registered in the Register of Crofts.

As from the effective date of 25 June 2007 every holding entered in the Register of Crofts on that date which has been so entered for a continuous period of at least 20 years ending with that date (and in respect of which no application or reference seeking a declaration or order that the holding is not a croft is on that date pending before any court) is a croft.

Likewise as from the date 20 years after registration, every holding entered in the Register of Crofts for a continuous period of 20 years ending after the effective date of 25 June 2007 (and in respect of which no application or reference seeking a declaration or order that the holding is not a croft is at the end of that period pending before any court) is a croft.

From the Crofting Commission Annual Report & Accounts 2017/18 it can be gleaned that there are 20,777 crofts entered on the Register of Crofts of which 14,968 are tenanted and the remainder (5,809) are owned.

This can be broken down within various areas as follows:-

Area	Tenanted	Owned
Argyll & Bute	458	351
Highland	6,283	3,670
Western Isles	6,072	234
North Ayrshire	0	1
Orkney	64	393
Shetland	2,091	1,160
Totals	**14,968**	**5,809**

There has been a dramatic increase in recent years in the number of crofts listed on the Register of Crofts due to that register now including 'deemed crofts' which are for all intents and purposes simply shares in the common grazing (Chapter 8).

It is possible to create new crofts (Chapter 15).

You will only find crofts in the crofting counties or in any area outwith the crofting counties which has, by order made by statutory instrument, been designated by the Scottish Ministers as areas within which new crofts can be created.

The crofting counties are the former counties of Argyll, Caithness, Inverness, Orkney, Ross and Cromarty, Sutherland and Zetland (now Shetland).

With effect from 4 February 2010, the Scottish Ministers designated those parts of Highland local government area not already within the crofting counties; the local government area of Moray; in the local government area of Argyll and Bute the parishes of Kingarth, North Bute and Rothesay; and in the local government area of North Ayrshire the islands of Arran (including Holy Island and Pladda), Great Cumbrae and Little Cumbrae as areas within which new crofts can be created.

The term crofter is commonly used to refer to both a crofting tenant and an owner-occupier crofter. However, in the 1993 Act "crofter" means the tenant of a croft. The term "owner-occupier crofter" was first introduced into law by the 2010 Act.

A person is an owner-occupier crofter if all of the following three conditions are satisfied:-

1. That person is the owner of a croft;

2. That the person:

   (a) was the crofter of the croft at the time of acquiring it (or is such a crofter's successor in title);

   (b) acquired title to the croft as the nominee of a crofter (or is such a nominee's successor in title); or

   (c) purchased the croft from the landlord who constituted it as a new croft (Chapter 15) or their successor in title (or is such a purchaser's successor in title).

3. That the croft has not been let to any person as a crofter either by virtue of the owner-occupier crofters letting procedures, or otherwise at any time since (a) it was acquired from the landlord; or (b) constituted as a new croft.

The definition of an owner-occupier crofter is somewhat convoluted and it is not uncommon to find people that you would expect to be owner-occupier crofters falling outside that definition and as a result not being entitled to claim crofting grants (Chapter 11) that an owner-occupier crofter or crofting tenant can claim. There is a way and means to convert a non owner-occupier crofter into an owner-occupier crofter (Chapter 7).

In the Crofting Commission Annual Report & Accounts 2017/18 it is stated that 65% of crofters are male and 35% are female.

The 2017/18 Report for some reason did not include average ages of crofters whereas the previous 2016/17 Report did. That earlier Report disclosed that the average age of a crofter is:-

0 – 20 years old	0.23%
21 – 40 years old	10.94%
41 – 60 years old	39.83%
61 – 80 years old	39.36%
81 + years old	9.64%

CHAPTER THREE
CROFTING COMMISSION

The Crofting Commission (formerly the Crofters Commission before the 2010 Act) based in Inverness regulates crofting (crofting.scotland.gov.uk). Six commissioners from geographic areas in the crofting counties are elected by crofters and three are appointed by the Scottish Ministers. One commissioner (the "convener") chairs the Commission. The convener is appointed by the Scottish Ministers although they can (and so far have done so only once) delegate selection of the convener to the Commission. The first three conveners of the new Crofting Commission were Susan Walker (2012 – 2015), Colin Kennedy (2015 – 2017) and Rod Mackenzie (2017 – present). The Commission is supported by a staff of some 59, led by a Chief Executive (currently Bill Barron).

The Crofting Commission operate independently of the Scottish Government as a non-departmental public body but one for which Scottish Ministers are ultimately responsible. They must discharge their functions in accordance with such directions of a general or specific character as may from time to time be given to them in writing by the Scottish Ministers.

The Crofting Commission have the general functions of (i) regulating crofting; (ii) reorganising crofting; (iii) promoting the interests of crofting; and (iv) keeping under review matters relating to crofting. They also, in addition, have such other functions as may be conferred on them under the 1993 Act or under any other enactment.

Regulatory applications (for example by a crofter to assign their croft tenancy, sub-let their croft, grant a short lease, obtain consent to be absent, apportion common grazings, subdivide their croft or remove part of their croft from crofting tenure through decrofting) require to be submitted to the Crofting Commission for approval.

Many straightforward applications are delegated to officials to process and only in contentious cases will Commissioners require to get involved in the decision making.

The Crofting Commission must make an annual report, on the exercise by them of their functions, to the Scottish Ministers. They must also prepare and submit to the Scottish Ministers, for approval, a plan setting out their policy on how they propose to exercise their functions.

The Crofting Commission, in exercising their functions, must have regard to any approved plan.

The Scottish Land Court (Chapter 4) may have regard to any such plan when considering an appeal against (a) any decision, determination or direction of; or (b) the imposition of a condition by, the Crofting Commission on an application made to them under the 1993 Act.

The first five years of the Crofting Commission (after the name change from Crofters Commission brought about by the 2010 Act) were marred with controversy over not being able to process decrofting applications on owner-occupied crofts, the sacking of common grazings committees and other issues (croftinglawblog.com).

Fergus Ewing MSP, Cabinet Secretary for the Rural Economy, asked Scott-Moncrieff, business advisers and accountants, to conduct a review into the Governance of the Crofting Commission, which culminated in their report of February 2017. This report highlighted a range of areas that needed urgent action including:-

- Governance standards, procedures and other arrangements, at both executive and non-executive levels, to underpin effective decision-making, particularly in relation to the Bohuntin, Upper Coll and Mangersta Common Grazings cases [Note: The review did not look at the regulatory decisions themselves].

- Arrangements for handling conflicts of interest.

- Ensuring that capacity building and development needs of Board members are met and that the necessary training is provided.

Fergus Ewing, said:-

> *"This review highlights notable and worrying failures in the governance of the Crofting Commission which must be improved immediately. That is why I have asked the new Chief Executive to urgently prepare an action plan to take this forward.*
>
> *Crofting is an integral part of Scottish rural life and it is essential that it has an effective regulator. This review, and the action plan which will follow, must help to deliver the necessary changes and ensure the Commission is able to lead the crofting industry forward."*

However, the election/appointment of new commissioners in 2017 and the appointment of a new convener ushered in a sea change and, so far, a much calmer and more sensible approach to crofting regulation.

CHAPTER FOUR
SCOTTISH LAND COURT

The Scottish Land Court (scottish-land-court.org.uk) deals with disputes concerning crofts.

Under the 1993 Act the Court has, for example, jurisdiction:-

- to determine whether a holding is a croft within the terms of the 1993 Act;
- to determine the extent and boundaries of a croft;
- to determine a fair rent for the croft;
- to authorise a landlord to resume (that is, to take back) croft land or common grazings for a reasonable purpose;
- to determine rights of access;
- to authorise a crofter to acquire a heritable title to their croft from their landlord;
- to deal with appeals from decisions or determinations of the Crofting Commission.

Following the passing of the 2010 Act, the Court now also has jurisdiction to deal with challenges to the first registration of crofts or common grazings in the Crofting Register.

The Court is based in Edinburgh but will usually hold hearings near to the location of the croft that is the subject of the dispute (perhaps in a local Sheriff Court, public hall, community centre or hotel). They have even been known to convene in a croft house.

The provisions relating to the Court can be found in the Scottish Land Court Act 1993 as amended.

The Court has a Chairman, who has the same status as a Court of Session judge, a Deputy Chairman, who is an advocate, and two Members of Court, who are experienced in farming and crofting matters.

The current Chairman of the Court is Lord Minginish, who was installed on 17 October 2014, following the retirement of Lord McGhie, who had been Chairman since 1996. The Deputy Chairman of the Court is Iain F Maclean, who took up office on 14 September 2015. The present agricultural Members of the Court are John Smith, who was appointed in March 2006, and Tom Campbell, who joined the Court in February 2016. The Gaelic-speaking member of the Court, as required by the Scottish Land Court Act 1993, is Lord Minginish.

The Court has a Principal Clerk, currently Alison Irving, and a number of administrative staff.

The Court may decide that a case is suitable to be dealt with by one of the expert Members, in which case it will delegate the case to that Member. The Member will then decide the case with the assistance of the Principal Clerk. A decision by a Member can be appealed to the full court.

Court staff, with the assistance of Court Members where necessary, give careful attention to the best way of dealing with all disputes that come into the Court. The Court tries to avoid undue formality and expense. Where possible, they dispose of matters in writing on the basis of written submissions. The Members will often inspect the land in question to be sure that they have a proper understanding of the nature of the dispute.

By tradition, the Court combines a proper judicial approach to resolving disputes with an ease of access to litigants. In other words, it is fairly formal when necessary in the interests of justice and fairness, but relatively informal wherever possible. It is formal at times because when important decisions are being taken, it is right that parties should know where they stand.

The Court has been referred to in the past as being "user friendly". More recently, Jim McPherson, a Caithness crofter, described the Court as "the jewel in the crown of crofting".

The current rules of procedure of the Court ('Scottish Land Court Rules') can be found in the Schedule to the Rules of the Scottish Land Court Order 2014 (SSI 2014/229). A useful guide to the Court's practice and procedure is given by Keith Graham in 'Scottish Land Court Practice and Procedure' (1993), although that book does predate the Court's current rules.

An application to the Court should be made by using one of their prescribed forms which are available to download from their website.

The Court normally acknowledges applications within one week of receipt. The Court may ask for further details or clarification if the application is in any way unclear or incomplete.

The Court will then notify the details of the application to the other party (or parties), and will invite them to give their response:

that is, their answers to the matters raised in the application. Normally, the Court will then ask the applicant to give a reply to any responses received. This process may be repeated until the stage is reached when the application is ready to be heard.

You will find reported decisions of the Scottish Land Court in one of four sets of reports set out below. Modern reports are in the Scottish Land Court's own series or on their website, and you can obtain copies of decisions from the Court. Some are reported in the Scots Law Times. The reporting of older decisions is a little more complicated.

Scottish Land Court Reports 1913–1963

Decisions of the Land Court were published as a supplement to the Scottish Law Review and Reports of Sheriff Court Cases and the published decisions in each year were bound as the Scottish Land Court Reports. The reports date from 1913 to 1963. To refer to a particular decision it is normally sufficient to quote the year and the page number, abbreviating Scottish Land Court Reports to SLCR, thus: Balfour v Couper 1963 SLCR 13. However, since 1913 variations have been used. Scott in the 'Law of Smallholdings' (1933) refers to cases simply by their volume number, for example, Hart v Campbell 10 SLCR 13 = 1922 SLCR 13, whilst MacCuish and Flyn in 'Crofting Law' (1990) refer to cases with their date in brackets and the volume number, thus: Falconer v Murray (1913) 1 SLCR 53. Flyn and Graham in 'Crofting Law' (2017) remove the brackets and the volume number and refer to cases just by their year and page number, thus: Adamson v Sharp's Trs 1917 SLCR 76.

Scottish Land Court Reports 1982 to date

Since 1982 the Land Court has produced its own volumes of reported decisions each year and these are referred to simply by the year and the page number, thus: Luss Estates Co v Colquhoun 1982 SLCR 1.

You will find the headnotes for these reported cases from 1982 to 2008 in the Digest of Cases on the Court's website.

Scots Law Times 1964 to date

From 1964 some decisions of the Court have also been reported in the Scots Law Times in a section dealing with Land Court cases. The cases are reported as, for example, Macdonald v Greig 1964 SLT (Land Ct) 5.

Appendices to the Scottish Land Court Reports 1912–1981

In terms of section 18 of the 1886 Act, the original Crofters Commission was obliged to make a report to the Secretary of State for Scotland as to its proceedings, and every report was to be presented to Parliament. That particular section was applied to the Scottish Land Court in terms of section 28 of the 1911 Act and accordingly each year the Court is still required to present a report as to its proceedings to Parliament. From 1912–1981, the Court published appendices to the Annual Reports in which it detailed in table form certain categories of case, for example, fair rents fixed for crofts or compensation awarded for permanent improvements but in addition various decisions of the Court were reported in these appendices. Cases referred to in these appendices are normally cited as, for example, Bell v Forestry Commission 1980 SLCR App 116.

Significant Decisions 2007 to date

The Court publishes reports of cases dealing with significant legal issues or which are of general interest on their website.

Previous Applications

The Court has in store all the previous applications made to the Court, and the applications to the original Crofters Commission from 1886 to 1911. The Court maintains an index of these decisions based on the name of the agricultural holding or the name of the croft or crofting township. An examination of the records will show whether the Court or the original Crofters Commission has ever considered an application relating to a particular holding or croft. These earlier applications can be a valuable source of information; for example, in determining the boundaries of a croft.

The administrative staff of the Court are regularly asked to check these records for old applications relating to a particular place, and for this service they charge a search fee. Should any photocopies of old applications be required an additional charge is made for the photocopies.

For an interesting and entertaining account of the history of the Scottish Land Court see 'No Ordinary Court: 100 years of the Scottish Land Court' (2012).

CHAPTER FIVE
REGISTER OF CROFTS AND CROFTING REGISTER

On 28 August 2017 the Register of Crofts went live online via the Crofting Commission (crofting.scotland.gov.uk/register-of-crofts). Now this is not to be confused with the Crofting Register which was already live online via Registers of Scotland (crofts.ros.gov.uk/register/home) and was introduced under the 2010 Act.

The Register of Crofts is the old register held and maintained by the Crofting Commission which is not necessarily authoritative but based on information supplied to it. Unlike the Crofting Register it is not map based.

Until crofts are registered on the Crofting Register information on the Register of Crofts will remain important and even after registration in the Crofting Register there may be information on the Register of Crofts about a croft that you will not find on the Crofting Register.

There are certain trigger events that result in having to register a croft in the map-based Crofting Register held by Registers of Scotland. These are mostly linked to regulatory applications to the Crofting Commission such as to decroft or assign.

The purchase by a crofting tenant of a croft from their landlord does not trigger registration in the Crofting Register (this is believed to have been a mistake in the drafting of the 2010 Act that is likely to be rectified in future crofting law reform).

However, the subsequent sale of such a purchased croft will trigger registration in the Crofting Register.

Crofts can be voluntarily registered in the Crofting Register without waiting for a trigger event to happen.

The fee for registration and for subsequent updates to the registration is £90 per application to register/update.

Applications must be submitted via the Crofting Commission to Registers of Scotland.

The Crofting Commission were registering common grazings in the Crofting Register but that came to a halt when they ran out of funding specifically given to them by the Scottish Government for that task. They subsequently started the process again on a more limited scale than before, but this time funded from savings made elsewhere within their budget. However, it is understood that they are not currently actively pursuing the registration of common grazings.

Following registration in the Register of Crofts there is a nine-month period to apply to the Scottish Land Court for an order that the entry in the Crofting Register be removed or modified.

The Court has the power on "cause shown" to deal with any application made after that period. However, in one case, where the boundaries of a croft had been wrongly registered to include part of a neighbouring croft and the neighbouring crofter had simply been too busy with other things to deal with a challenge timeously, the Land Court, in refusing the challenge made, observed:-

> *"In our opinion 'cause shown' requires something which justifies or at least excuses the failure to make the application timeously. Illness and consequent inability to deal with the matter would be an example. If merely being too busy with other things was to be an adequate reason the time limit would be rendered nugatory. It also has to be noted in the present context that a time period of nine months for bringing a challenge is a very long one; far longer than most statutorily prescribed time limits for bringing appeals."*

The Keeper of the Registers of Scotland may rectify the Crofting Register, to correct a mistake in an application for registration, on the application for rectification by the person who made the original application. It is, however, not always that original applicant who has a real interest to ensure rectification, but it could be some third party who is affected by an erroneous registration.

Rectification is also available at the instance of the Crofting Commission in relation to a mistake made by them in forwarding the application to Registers of Scotland. In addition, if a mistake was made by the Keeper of the Registers of Scotland when making up or amending the registration schedule then the Keeper may, of her own volition, rectify that mistake.

If rectification is necessary at the instance of the Crofting Commission or Registers of Scotland to correct mistakes made by them then they are liable for the costs involved including those incurred by any person to ensure rectification.

A person who suffers loss as a result of (a) a mistake in the register made by the Keeper when making up or amending a registration schedule or making consequential amendments in the register, the correction of which would require rectification of the register; (b) a rectification of the register to correct such a mistake; (c) the refusal by the Keeper to make such a rectification, (d) the loss or destruction of any document while lodged with the Keeper; or (e) a mistake in any certificate of registration or in any information given by the Keeper in writing, is entitled to be indemnified by the Keeper in respect of that loss.

A person aggrieved by any act or omission of the Keeper may appeal any issue or fact of law arising from that act or omission to the Scottish Land Court. On such an appeal the Court may order the Keeper to take such remedial action as the order may specify, including action to rectify the register.

CHAPTER SIX
STATUTORY CONDITIONS, LANDLORD'S RESERVED RIGHTS, RESIDENCY AND CULTIVATION OBLIGATIONS

There are various fundamental rights and responsibilities affecting the relationship between a crofting tenant and a landlord and obligations that must be adhered to whether you are a crofting tenant or an owner-occupier crofter.

Statutory Conditions

A crofting tenant must abide by the statutory conditions which are:-

- The crofter shall pay their rent at the terms at which it is due and payable.
- The crofter shall not, except in accordance with the provisions of the 1993 Act, execute any deed purporting to assign their tenancy.
- The crofter shall provide such fixed equipment on their croft as may be necessary to enable them to cultivate the croft.
- The crofter shall not, to the prejudice of the interest of the landlord, injure the croft (a) by allowing the dilapidation of buildings; (b) where the croft is cultivated, by allowing,

after relevant notice, the deterioration of the soil; or (c) where the croft is put to some other purposeful use, by actings prejudicial to that use being actings carried out after relevant notice ["relevant notice" means notice given by the landlord to the crofter not to do, or not to allow, a particular thing or not to engage in a particular course of conduct (being a thing or course of conduct specified in the notice and relevant to the deterioration or prejudice in question)].

- The crofter shall not sublet their croft or any part thereof otherwise than with the consent in writing of the Crofting Commission and in accordance with such conditions (which shall not include conditions relating to rent) as the Crofting Commission in giving their consent may impose. This does not, however, debar a crofter from subletting any dwelling-house or other building forming part of their croft to holiday visitors.

- The crofter shall be responsible for ensuring, where the croft is sublet, that the subtenant adheres to the statutory conditions.

- The crofter shall not, except in accordance with the provisions of the 1993 Act, divide their croft.

- The crofter shall not, without the consent in writing of the landlord, erect or suffer to be erected on the croft any dwelling-house otherwise than in substitution for a dwelling-house which at the commencement of the 1993 Act was already on the croft: Provided that, if at the commencement of the 1993 Act there was no dwelling-house on the croft, the crofter may erect one dwelling-house thereon.

- The crofter shall not violate any written condition signed by them for the protection of the interest of the landlord or of neighbouring crofters which is legally applicable to the croft and which the Scottish Land Court shall find to be reasonable.
- The crofter shall not do any act whereby they become apparently insolvent within the meaning of the Bankruptcy (Scotland) Act 2016.
- The crofter shall not on their croft, without the consent in writing of the landlord, open any house for the sale of intoxicating liquors.

Landlord's Reserved Rights

A landlord has various reserved rights over tenanted croft land. As part of the statutory conditions a crofter shall permit the landlord or any person authorised by the landlord to enter upon the croft for the purpose of exercising (subject always to the payment of such compensation as in case of dispute the Scottish Land Court may find to be reasonable in respect of any damage done or occasioned thereby) any of the following rights, and shall not obstruct the landlord or any person authorised by them in the exercise of any of such rights, that is to say:-

- mining or taking minerals, or digging or searching for minerals;

- quarrying or taking stone, marble, gravel, sand, clay, slate or other workable mineral;
- using for any estate purpose any springs of water rising on the croft and not required for the use thereof;
- cutting or taking timber or peats, excepting timber and other trees planted by the crofter or any of their predecessors in the tenancy, or which may be necessary for ornament or shelter, and excepting also such peats as may be required for the use of the croft;
- opening or making roads, fences, drains and water courses;
- passing and re-passing to and from the shore of the sea or any loch with or without vehicles for the purpose of exercising any right of property or other right belonging to the landlord;
- viewing or examining at reasonable times the state of the croft and all buildings or improvements thereon;
- hunting, shooting, fishing or taking game or fish, wild birds or vermin.

However, nothing specified above in respect of reserved rights shall be held to allow, or require the crofter to allow, the landlord, or any person authorised by the landlord, to exercise unreasonably a right enjoyed by virtue of those reserved rights.

Residency and Cultivation Obligations

A crofting tenant and/or an owner-occupier crofter is obliged to be ordinarily resident on or within 32 kilometres of the croft.

They must not misuse or neglect the croft.

They must cultivate the croft; or put it to another purposeful use, so that every part of the croft which is capable of being cultivated or put to another purposeful use either is cultivated or is put to such use.

They must keep the croft in a fit state for cultivation (except in so far as the use of the croft for another purposeful use is incompatible with the croft being kept in such a state).

"Cultivate" includes the use of the croft for horticulture or for any purpose of husbandry, including the keeping or breeding of livestock, poultry or bees; the growing of fruit, vegetables and the like; and the planting of trees and use of the land as woodlands.

"Purposeful use" means any planned and managed use which does not adversely affect the croft; the public interest; the interests of the landlord or (if different) the owner; or the use of adjacent land.

The Crofting Commission can take action concerning suspected breaches of these conditions which, if not remedied, could result in the termination of a tenancy or an owner-occupier crofter being compelled to let their croft.

CHAPTER SEVEN
CROFT PURCHASE

There are different circumstances that will apply to a croft purchase depending on the status of the croft and the relative crofter. It could be (i) the purchase of a croft tenancy from an existing crofting tenant; or (ii) the purchase of an owner-occupied croft; or (iii) the purchase of the landlord's interest in a vacant croft; or (iv) the purchase of a croft from the landlord by the crofting tenant. We will look at each in turn and then consider finding a croft to purchase and the vexed question of crofting mortgages.

Purchasing a Crofting Tenancy

Having located a crofting tenancy to purchase the intending purchaser will need to instruct their solicitor to submit an offer to purchase the tenancy to the current crofting tenant's solicitors.

The transfer of the tenancy is referred to as an "assignation", the current tenant is the "assignor" and the new tenant is the "assignee".

The offer to purchase will be subject to obtaining the consent of the Crofting Commission.

It is usual for the purchase price to be consigned with the assignee's solicitor upon conclusion of the contract to purchase the tenancy and pending the consent of the Crofting Commission being obtained.

An application form requires completion and submission to the Crofting Commission by the assignor seeking approval to the assignation of the tenancy. The proposed assignee will have to complete Section 5 of the application form with their details and information concerning their proposed residency on the croft, cultivation and maintenance of the croft, and whether they intend to put the croft or any part of it to a purposeful use other than cultivation (e.g. tourist development, livery or a renewable energy project).

The assignee will also be asked to provide information on what experience and/or skills they have to implement their plans for working and maintaining the land, including non-agricultural experience and skills.

If the assignee is currently the owner, owner-occupier crofter, tenant crofter or subtenant of any other croft or agricultural land they will be asked for information concerning that land and how they cultivate or otherwise use it.

The assignor is required to advertise in the local press that they are making the application and they must notify their landlord in writing, as well as the owner of the common grazing if including grazing shares.

If the assignor has not already done so, they will be required to register the croft with Registers of Scotland in the Crofting Register.

Providing the croft is registered in the Crofting Register, the Crofting Commission aim to take a decision on the application within 16 weeks. If the croft is not registered, they cannot take a decision on the application until this has happened.

There is a 42-day appeal period once the application is granted and settlement of the purchase would normally only take place after that period has expired and no appeal has been lodged with the Scottish Land Court.

Purchasing an Owner-Occupied Croft

Having located an owner-occupied croft to purchase the intending purchaser will need to instruct their solicitor to submit an offer to purchase.

The consent of the Crofting Commission to the purchase of an owner-occupied croft is not required.

Accordingly, purchasing an owner-occupied croft should be a more straight forward and quicker process.

If, however, grazing shares are included that are a tenanted (as opposed to being a heritable) right then these will be classed as a 'deemed croft' and will require to be assigned using the same process as purchasing a croft tenancy outlined above.

If the owner-occupied croft has not already been registered in the Crofting Register then the purchase will trigger first registration.

It is not possible to purchase part of an owner-occupied croft without first having it formally divided by application to the Crofting Commission. Any purchase without such formal division will be null and void. So it is important to make sure that the whole croft is being purchased.

Purchasing the Landlord's interest in a Vacant Croft

If the croft is owned but does not fall within the strict statutory definition of an owner-occupied croft then the purchase will be of the landlord's interest in a vacant croft. The purchaser will not become an owner-occupier crofter. Thus they will not be entitled to claim grants that an owner-occupier crofter could claim.

There are, however, ways and means to turn such a croft into an owner-occupied croft. This would involve granting a tenancy with the consent of the Crofting Commission to someone that the owner knows and trusts. Once they become the tenant they would exercise their right to purchase the croft and they would become owner-occupier. They could then convey that owner-occupied croft back to the original owner who would then be an owner-occupier crofter.

The Bill Team are currently considering a quicker fix that would allow, by way of future legislation, the Crofting Commission to grant owner-occupier status in such circumstances on an application being made to them.

Purchasing from a Landlord

A crofting tenant has an absolute right to purchase their croft house and garden ground and the ability to purchase all or any part of their croft land.

If a landlord is unwilling to negotiate the terms of a sale a crofting tenant may apply to the Scottish Land Court for an order authorising them to purchase the croft or part of the croft.

A landlord can block the sale of croft land (but not of the croft house and garden ground) through the Scottish Land Court if they can prove a sale would cause them a substantial degree of hardship and/or be substantially detrimental to the interests of sound management of their estate.

A purchase will be at 15 times the rent currently being paid or a fair rent fixed, failing agreement, by the Scottish Land Court. A crofting tenant and a landlord can always agree a rent and often will do so. That agreed rent will then effectively stand for seven years or for such longer period as may have been agreed upon between the crofting tenant and the landlord. During that period the rent cannot be altered by the Scottish Land Court.

The landlord is entitled to the grant of a standard security by the purchasing crofter over the croft in their favour for clawback purposes. In simple terms this entitles them to receive from the crofter 50% of the value of the croft or part thereof if sold by the crofter within 10 years of purchase. This does not apply to the croft house and garden ground or to transfers of the croft land to a member of the crofter's family (as defined by the 1993 Act).

A Landlord can seek and is generally entitled (for a period of not less than 20 years) to a lease back of the shooting rights over or the fishing rights pertaining to the croft on a sale of it.

Finding a Croft to Purchase

The Scottish Crofting Federation (SCF) maintains a register of available crofts for sale.

Their list is updated on a monthly basis, with details of available crofts gathered from a wide range of estate agents and websites. It is then up to a prospective purchaser to research the suitability of the croft for their needs and get in touch directly with the appropriate selling agent. With individuals also listing crofts themselves for sale locally and in the press, this will not be a fully comprehensive list of what is out there – but it will be a helpful start on the road to finding an ideal croft. The list published by the SCF as at 14 February 2019 had 196 crofts on it available for purchase.

Members of the SCF can request to be added to the e-mail distribution list for the Available Crofts Update.

Other sources will be local estate agent's websites, for sale sections in local newspapers and hspc.co.uk (for crofts around Inverness – estate agents on the Isle of Skye, Western Isles, Orkney, Shetland, Caithness and Sutherland tend not to use the Highland Solicitors Property Centre). Crofts might also be listed for sale on national property portals such as zoopla.co.uk, rightmove.co.uk and onthemarket.com. Word of mouth, investigating the ownership of derelict crofts and approaching the owner directly or placing a "croft wanted" advert in a local newspaper are other possible ways to find an available croft to purchase.

The value of a croft varies wildly depending on size, location and whether it is a bare land croft or one with a croft house and/or other buildings on it. The list of available crofts for sale published by the SCF as at 14 February 2019 has prices on it ranging from £10,000 to £635,000.

Croft Mortgages

At the moment it is only possible to borrow money by way of secured funding (a mortgage) from a bank or other lender on land that has been removed from crofting tenure by decrofting or resumption.

Thus if a croft that includes a decrofted house is being purchased then the purchaser should be able to borrow secured finance based on the value of the house alone but excluding the value of the croft. They might be able to borrow up to 90% of the value of the house but are unlikely at present to get a lender who will loan more than that.

The purchaser will therefore need hard cash for the balance required to fund any purchase over and above what lending they may be able to get.

The purchaser may, of course, be able to get an unsecured loan to assist or tap into the 'bank of mum and dad'.

The Bill Team is looking at the question of mortgages over croft land. This was considered in 2010 and formed part of the reform Bill at that time but was not enacted in the 2010 Act. This is now generally thought to have been a mistake and there is renewed support for its introduction in the next crofting Act.

Strangely in 2010 the Scottish Government only considered mortgages over tenanted crofts and not over owner-occupied ones. The Bill Team is considering mortgages over both.

In the future therefore it may be possible to get secured finance to purchase a croft.

CHAPTER EIGHT
COMMON GRAZINGS COMMITTEES, GRAZING SHARES, APPORTIONMENTS AND DEEMED CROFTS

A croft may come with a share in the common grazing. In Shetland a common grazing is called a scattald.

If a croft is held in tenancy any shares in the common grazing will be part and parcel of that tenancy.

If a croft is owner-occupied then the common grazing shares are likely to be held in tenancy as a 'deemed croft' but could have been included in the title as a heritable right.

The position of the Keeper of the Registers of Scotland in regard to common grazings is that it is not an ownership right and if expressed in such terms will not be disclosed on a Title Sheet as a pertinent to the croft. However, if a right in common to land (that happens to be common grazing) is conveyed then it will fall to be dealt with in the same manner as any other shared ownership plot.

Any right in pasture or grazing can be deemed to form part of the croft as an ancillary incorporeal right that is a pertinent. Unlike a registrable long lease, a crofting tenancy is not a leasehold interest that is (a) registrable or (b) entered into the Title Sheet of the ownership interest in the Schedule of Leases. Registers of Scotland therefore see it as an 'off register' right, and not one which would be shown in the Title Sheet.

The submission of a Disposition for registration which included, in addition to the croft being registered, a share in common grazings would not be an issue. The Title Sheet however will remain silent on the ownership of a right in the common grazings. The registered deed would enter the archive record of Registers of Scotland, and could be viewed as part of the register to offer reassurance that the share in the common grazings had been transferred as part of the Disposition. It should be noted however that the archive record is a repository of documents supporting the accuracy of the Land Register, and as shares in common grazings are an 'off register' right it can offer no assurances as to anything that may happen to that right off register.

If common grazing shares have been 'separated' from the croft and became a 'deemed croft' then they can be transferred independently of the croft. The Bill Team are currently looking at the question of attaching such shares to the croft as part of possible future crofting law reform.

The souming is the extent of a shareholder's individual right to graze stock on a common grazing. This may for example be a specified number of sheep and/or cows. It also quantifies the shareholder's right to share in any compensation received by the common grazing, for example on resumption (Chapter 9) or under a scheme for development (Chapter 10).

There may be a grazings committee in place to manage the common grazings with a clerk and chairperson. If so the common grazings will be regulated and will have a set of Grazing Regulations governing its use. Committees can amend or adopt new regulations to assist in the proper management and administration of their common grazings, subject to approval by the Crofting Commission.

The Crofting Commission Annual Report & Accounts 2017/18 discloses the following facts about common grazings:-

Area	**Total Common Grazings**	**Committees in Office**
Argyll & Bute	61	8
Highland	539	237
Western Isles	295	177
Orkney	9	1
Shetland	168	40
Totals	**1,072**	**463**

Grazings committees must report every five years to the Crofting Commission on (a) the condition of the common grazing; (b) the condition of every croft of a crofter sharing in the grazing; (c) the condition of every owner-occupied croft of an owner-occupier crofter sharing in the grazing; (d) any other matter the Crofting Commission may require.

In 2016 there was much controversy over the question of retention and distribution of funds by grazings committees and the Crofting Commission's ever-changing stance on that following the dismissal by them of three grazings committees. You can read all about it at: croftinglawblog.com/101-blog-posts-on-the-common-clearances

The question of possible personal liability of members of a grazings committee has been raised with the Bill Team as an issue. At the moment that is considered a second phase problem to be dealt with during the next Parliamentary term. In the meantime the Crofting Commission have suggested, in their 'Guidance for Common Grazings' (February 2019), that a grazings committee may wish to consider whether they should have appropriate insurance cover to deal with any problems or claims that may arise because of activities on the common grazing. They have further suggested that the cost of any such insurance should be met by all shareholders.

A shareholder can seek to apportion their shares or part thereof in a common grazing for their exclusive use by application to the Crofting Commission. Such an application will trigger first registration in the Crofting Register or be an event affecting a registered croft that must be registered in that register.

A crofter has the right to purchase an apportionment only if it is contiguous or adjacent to their croft and they have exercised the right to purchase at the same time as purchasing the croft tenancy.

CHAPTER NINE DECROFTING AND RESUMPTION

Decrofting and resumption are processes that remove land from crofting tenure.

A crofting tenant or owner-occupier crofter seeking to remove land from crofting tenure can do so by way of an application to decroft via the Crofting Commission.

A landlord, on the other hand, will have to resume land from crofting tenure via an application to the Scottish Land Court. Usually a crofter's expenses will require to be met by the landlord (even where a crofter opposes the application and the landlord is successful). On resumption the crofter will receive one-half of the value of the land resumed as compensation. If the crofter is in agreement to resumption proceeding the landlord should get them to sign a minute of consent to be lodged with the application to the Scottish Land Court thus simplifying the process and making it non-contentious.

Decrofting or resumption is usually done for the purposes of a proposed development such as the construction of a dwelling house or other building. The Crofting Commission and the Land Court will want to see the grant of planning permission for the development in question.

Resumption must be for a "reasonable purpose" which is defined in the 1993 Act to include:-

(a) the using, letting or disposing of the land proposed to be resumed for:-

- the building of dwellings;
- small allotments;
- harbours, piers, boat shelters or other like buildings;
- churches or other places of religious worship;
- schools;
- halls or community centres;
- planting;
- roads practicable for vehicular traffic from the croft or township to the public road or to the seashore;
- the generation of energy; or
- any other purpose likely to provide employment for crofters and others in the locality;

(b) the protection of an ancient monument or other object of historical or archaeological interest from injury or destruction.

Both decrofting and resumption will trigger first registration in the Crofting Register or be an event affecting a registered croft that must be registered in that register.

CHAPTER TEN
SCHEMES FOR DEVELOPMENT

Schemes for Development are often utilised for renewable energy projects on croft land or common grazing (or land near to croft land or common grazings if rights and liabilities in relation to the croft land or common grazings would be affected).

The Scottish Land Court might approve a scheme to allow such a project to proceed with appropriate compensation flowing (probably on an annual basis) throughout the duration of the scheme to the crofters affected.

They are often referred to as "section 19A" applications or intimations after the section of the 1993 Act inserted by the 2007 Act.

Other types of development could fall under this provision. For example, it is likely that what could be the UK's first spaceport would require Scottish Land Court approval via a Scheme for Development. This is because the proposed site for vertical rocket and satellite launches is on common grazing at A'Mhoine, Sutherland and is part of the Melness Crofting Estate.

If you have the consent of every person who has rights in, or over, croft land or a common grazing affected by a Scheme for Development, it is an "intimation" to the Scottish Land Court under the 1993 Act. If you don't then it is an "application". Each is processed slightly differently by the Scottish Land Court according to the provisions set out for each in section 19A.

There must be a scheme appended to the application or intimation detailing how the land will be developed and what recompense will be involved.

The party submitting the application or intimation, as the case may be, to the Scottish Land Court will be the landlord (or owner) of the land in question, or any person acting with their consent. Thus it would not be uncommon for the developer, with the consent of the landlord (or owner), to lodge the application or intimation with the Court.

Whoever the party so doing is they must also send a copy of the application or intimation to the Crofting Commission together with a copy of the appended scheme. In addition they must give public notification of the application or intimation.

Within 28 days after the public notification is given (including the day on which it is given):-

(i) the Crofting Commission; or

(ii) any other interested party,

may submit to the Scottish Land Court written objections, on one or more of the following grounds:-

(a) that the development is not for a reasonable purpose;

(b) that to carry out the development would be unfair to the crofting community;

(c) in the case of a submission by the Crofting Commission, that the scheme does not provide for there to be fair recompense to each member of the crofting community;

(d) in the case of a submission by any other interested party:-

(i) that to carry out the development would be unfair to the objector;

(ii) that the scheme does not provide for there to be fair recompense to the objector;

(e) that, were the development to be carried out, the crofting community would be unlikely to benefit financially;

(f) that, were the development to be carried out, any financial benefit to the crofting community would not be at least commensurate with any financial benefit which the members of that community might obtain on the development proceeding other than by virtue of section 19A of the 1993 Act.

The Scottish Land Court shall hear the objectors (if any) before determining whether to give consent to an application or, as the case may be, before determining whether to proceed as respects an intimation.

It has been held by the Scottish Land Court that section 19A of the 1993 Act is concerned with the protection of crofting interests, and not with the wider public interest, of which account is taken in the planning process, so that persons who were not themselves members of the crofting community could not be an "interested party" for the purposes of being an objector to an application or an intimation as the case may be.

Consent to an application is not to be given unless the Scottish Land Court is satisfied:-

(a) that the development is for a reasonable purpose (see Chapter 9 for what "reasonable purpose" includes);

(b) that to carry it out would not be unfair;

(c) that the scheme provides for there to be fair recompense to each member of the crofting community in the area affected by the development for the effects of the development (including, in relation to the croft land of each such member, recompense at least equivalent to the recompense which the member might be expected to have obtained had that croft land been resumed); and

(d) that, were the development carried out:-

(i) that community would be likely to benefit financially; and

(ii) such benefit would be at least commensurate with any financial benefit which the members of that community might obtain on the development proceeding other than by virtue of section 19A of the 1993 Act.

If the Scottish Land Court gives consent to an application or determines to proceed as respects an intimation, they shall advise the Crofting Commission of this and provide them with a copy of the scheme in accordance with which the development is to take place. The Crofting Commission shall then enter that copy in the Register of Crofts. When so entered the scheme, in so far as its terms so provide, becomes binding.

CHAPTER ELEVEN
CROFT HOUSE GRANT AND CROFTING AGRICULTURAL GRANT SCHEME

The current Croft House Grant provides grants from the Scottish Government for new houses and the rebuilding and renovation of existing croft houses (ruralpayments.org/publicsite/futures/topics/all-schemes/croft-house-grant-).

Grant levels vary depending on geographical area with a maximum grant of £28,000 for standard areas and £38,000 for a priority area (the more remote and fragile communities). The Scottish Government provide a map showing what is a priority area and what is a standard one.

In 2017/18 the Croft House Grant scheme received extra funding of £600,000, taking the total allocation to £2 million.

The Crofting Agricultural Grant Scheme (CAGS) provides grants to crofters to make improvements to their crofts and to help sustain their businesses (ruralpayments.org/publicsite/futures/topics/all-schemes/crofting-agricultural-grant-scheme).

The total amount of grant aid that can be applied for in any two-year period by an individual crofter for any one business cannot exceed £25,000.

Funding for eligible capital improvement works to grazings and infrastructure by groups of crofters cannot exceed £125,000 in any two-year period.

CHAPTER TWELVE
CROFT DIVISION, ENLARGEMENT AND EXCHANGE

A crofter cannot divide their croft unless they obtain the consent of the Crofting Commission.

Division, if approved by the Crofting Commission will result in a new croft or crofts being created by such division which will require to be registered in the Crofting Register.

After division, the rent payable for the new crofts (i.e. each of the crofts created by the division of the original croft) shall be that agreed between the landlord and tenant. Failing such agreement the rents will be as determined by the Scottish Land Court on an application being made to them by either the landlord or the tenant. The fees payable in connection with such an application to the Scottish Land Court require to be borne by the tenant.

It is worth mentioning again that it is not possible to purchase part of an owner-occupied croft without first having it formally divided by application to the Crofting Commission. Any purchase without such formal division will be null and void. So it is important to make sure that the whole croft is being purchased.

That covers reducing a croft's size by division. But what if you want to enlarge a croft?

Enlargement can happen where an owner of land which is not a croft and which does not form part of a croft agrees to grant a tenancy of that land to a crofter.

The owner and the crofter may apply jointly to the Crofting Commission for a direction that the land is to form part of a croft of which the crofter is tenant.

The Crofting Commission may make such a direction if they are satisfied that the enlargement of the croft (a) would be of benefit to the croft or the crofter; and (b) would not result in the area of the enlarged croft substantially exceeding 30 hectares.

The rent payable for the enlarged croft is the rent agreed by the landlord and the crofter.

If an enlargement is applied for in respect of an unregistered croft then this will trigger first registration. In relation to a registered croft any direction given by the Crofting Commission will expire after three months of the date it was made unless an application for registration of the enlargement of the croft is made before the expiry of that three-month period. The enlargement takes effect on the date of registration.

We have looked at dividing and enlarging crofts but what if you simply want to exchange crofts with another crofter?

A crofter may not exchange their croft (or any part of their croft) for another croft (or part of another croft) unless (a) they obtain the consent of the landlord and the Crofting Commission; (b) the exchanging crofters have the same landlord; and (c) that landlord is the owner of any common grazing in which the crofters share.

The Crofting Commission cannot give their consent unless they are satisfied that the consent of the landlord has been obtained.

If consent is applied for in respect of an unregistered croft then this will trigger first registration. In relation to a registered croft or any part thereof any consent given by the Crofting Commission will expire after three months of the date it was given unless an application for registration of the exchange of the croft is made before the expiry of that three-month period. The exchange takes effect on the date of registration.

CHAPTER THIRTEEN
SUBLETS AND SHORT LEASES (SHORT TERM LETS)

When speaking about a crofting tenant remaining as a tenant but allowing another person to tenant their croft (rather than transferring or assigning the tenancy to them) then we refer to a sublet. If an owner-occupied croft is let to a tenant for a period not exceeding 10 years then we refer to the grant of a short lease (also known as a "short term let").

Sublets

A crofter is entitled to sublet their croft, for a period not exceeding 10 years, without the consent of the landlord of the croft.

A crofter cannot, however, sublet their croft otherwise than with the consent in writing of the Crofting Commission and in accordance with such conditions (which shall not include conditions relating to rent) as the Crofting Commission in giving their consent may impose.

Any sublease of a croft granted by a crofter without the consent of the Crofting Commission is null and void. However, there is nothing in law debarring a crofter from subletting any dwelling-house or other building forming part of a croft to holiday visitors.

The Crofting Commission may, in giving their consent to a proposed sublease of a croft, impose such conditions (other than any relating to rent) as they may think fit.

Subletting a croft does not trigger first registration of a croft in the Crofting Register nor is it an event that must be registered affecting a registered croft.

The subtenant under a sublease of a croft shall not be held to be a crofter.

However, where under a sublease of any croft a right in any common grazing is let to the subtenant then the subtenant shall come in place of the crofter in relation to any matter which concerns such right, and any grazings regulations applicable to such common grazing shall apply to the subtenant accordingly.

The conditions of let must specify that the crofter shall give the subtenant not less than 6 months written notice of any intention to assign, exchange or divide the croft and that the sublease shall come to an end on such assignation, exchange or division.

Where the tenancy of a croft is terminated, any sublease of that croft subsisting immediately before the date of such termination shall come to an end on that date: Provided that where a sublease comes to an end in this manner the Crofting Commission may, on an application in that behalf made to them by the subtenant within one month or such longer period not exceeding 3 months as the Crofting Commission may in all the circumstances think reasonable from the date on which the sublease came to an end, make an order permitting the subtenant to remain in occupation of the croft for such period, not exceeding one year from the said date, and subject to such conditions, as may be specified in the order. No proceedings for the removal of the subtenant from the croft shall be taken by the owner of the croft before the expiry of the said period of one month or the said longer period or, if an application is made to the Crofting Commission by the subtenant within that period, before the date of the determination of the Crofting Commission on such application.

Where the tenancy of a croft is terminated by virtue of the death of the crofter, the Crofting Commission shall, as part of their consideration in determining whether to make an order and if so what period of occupation to permit (a) consult the deceased crofter's executor; and (b) have regard in particular to such hardship as might, according to what they decide, be occasioned to (i) the former subtenant; or (ii) an assignee or transferee of the interest of tenant.

Short Leases (Short Term Lets)

An owner-occupier crofter may not let the owner-occupier's croft (or any part of it) without the consent of the Crofting Commission.

The Crofting Commission may, in giving their consent to a proposed lease of an owner-occupied croft for a period not exceeding 10 years (called a "short lease" in crofting legislation but often referred to as a "short term let" by the Crofting Commission), impose such conditions (other than any relating to rent) as they consider appropriate.

A lease is void if it is granted (a) without the Crofting Commission's consent; and (b) in the case of a short lease, otherwise than in accordance with such conditions as the Crofting Commission may impose.

The Crofting Commission may terminate a short lease if (a) a condition imposed by them is breached; or (b) the tenant fails to comply with a condition of let (other than any relating to rent).

However, no consents are required to let any dwelling-house or other building forming part of an owner-occupied croft to holiday visitors.

Granting a short lease of an owner-occupied croft does not trigger first registration of the croft in the Crofting Register nor is it an event that must be registered affecting a registered croft.

The tenant under a short lease of an owner-occupied croft shall not be treated as a crofter.

However, where by virtue of a short lease a right in a common grazing is let to the tenant under the lease then that tenant comes into the place of the owner-occupier crofter in relation to any matter which concerns the right, and any grazings regulations applicable to the grazing apply to the tenant accordingly.

Owner-occupier crofters can, with the consent of the Crofting Commission, grant a crofting tenancy (as opposed to a short lease) to a third party. In such circumstances the owner-occupier crofter would become a landlord and the tenant would become a crofter. In those circumstances this will trigger first registration. In relation to a registered croft or any part thereof any consent given by the Crofting Commission will expire after three months of the date it was given unless an application for registration of the letting of the croft is made before the expiry of that three month period. The letting of the croft (or part of the croft) takes effect on the date of registration.

CHAPTER FOURTEEN
RENUNCIATION, TERMINATION OF TENANCIES AND COMPENSATION FOR IMPROVEMENTS

A crofter shall be entitled, on one year's notice in writing to the landlord, to renounce their tenancy as at any term of Whitsunday (28th May) or Martinmas (28th November).

If a crofter renounces their tenancy the landlord shall be entitled to set off all rent due or to become due against any sum found to be due by the landlord to the crofter by way of compensation for permanent improvements made on the croft.

When (a) one year's rent of a croft is unpaid, (b) a crofter has broken one or more of the statutory conditions (other than the condition as to payment of rent), or (c) a crofter has breached their duties in respect of residency and not to misuse or neglect their croft then the Scottish Land Court may, on the application of the landlord and after considering any objections stated by the crofter, make an order (i) terminating the tenancy; (ii) declaring the croft to be vacant; and (iii) for removal of the tenant from the croft.

If the crofter remedies the breaches then it is unlikely that the tenancy will be terminated.

Where a crofter has sublet the croft, the crofter is deemed to comply with the relevant duties (other than the duty not to misuse the croft) if the crofter's subtenant complies with the duties;

Where the Commission have granted consent for the crofter to be absent from the croft then the crofter is deemed to comply with the residency duty.

If a crofter is removed from their croft the landlord shall be entitled to set off all rent due or to become due against any sum found to be due by the landlord to the crofter for permanent improvements made on the croft.

Where a crofter renounces their tenancy or is removed from their croft or the interest of the tenant which is comprised in the estate of a deceased crofter is terminated (Chapter 17) the crofter or, as the case may be, the executor of the deceased crofter shall be entitled to compensation for any permanent improvement made on the croft. This is so if:-

(a) the improvement is suitable to the croft; and

(b) the improvement was executed or paid for by the crofter or, as the case may be, the deceased crofter, or any of the predecessors of the crofter or of the deceased crofter in the tenancy; and

(c) either the improvement was executed otherwise than in pursuance of a specific agreement in writing under which the crofter or, as the case may be, the deceased crofter was bound to execute the improvement or, if the improvement was executed in pursuance of such an agreement, the crofter has not received or, as the case may be, the deceased crofter did not receive and their executor has not received, by way of reduction of rent or otherwise, fair consideration for the improvement.

The amount of the compensation payable shall, failing agreement, be fixed by the Scottish Land Court.

"Permanent improvement" means:-

- Dwelling-house.
- Improvement works carried out in compliance with a notice of a final resolution served under Part IV of the Housing (Scotland) Act 1987 (repair of houses).
- Farm offices.
- Subsoil and other drains.
- Walls and fences.
- Deep trenching.
- Clearing the ground.
- Planting trees, other than forestry on common grazings.
- Making piers or landing stages.
- Roads practicable for vehicles from the croft to the public road or the sea shore.
- All other improvements which, in the judgment of the Scottish Land Court, will add to the value of the croft as an agricultural subject.

- Buildings or other structures erected on the croft for any subsidiary or auxiliary occupation.

Provided that no building or other structure erected on a croft shall be held to be a permanent improvement on the croft unless it is a fixture on the land.

CHAPTER FIFTEEN
FORMATION OF NEW CROFTS

We have already looked at the fact that a croft can only exist in the original crofting counties or areas added to those counties by order made by the Scottish Ministers by statutory instrument (Chapter 2).

Any land situated in those counties or additional areas can be constituted as a croft by the Crofting Commission on an application being made to them by the owner of the land in question.

Such an owner cannot apply if the land in question is an agricultural holding occupied by a tenant where (a) the tenancy is (i) a 1991 Act tenancy (within the meaning of the Agricultural Holdings (Scotland) Act 2003); or (ii) a short limited duration tenancy, limited duration tenancy, modern limited duration tenancy or repairing tenancy (within the meaning of that Act); or (b) it is competent for the tenant to make an application themselves, if the written agreement of the tenant has not been obtained.

If, however, such a tenant consents and the Crofting Commission decide to constitute the holding as a croft then that tenant shall be entitled (unless not a natural person) to be registered as its crofting tenant.

If a tenant of any holding situated in those additional areas wishes that holding to be constituted as a croft, they can make application to the Crofting Commission for them to do so. They must, however, be a natural person and any fixed equipment on the holding as is necessary to enable the tenant to cultivate the croft cannot have been provided by the landlord. Any such application must be accompanied by a certificate of the Scottish Land Court to the effect that the Court is satisfied that, as at the date of the certificate:-

(a) the tenancy of the holding is one to which (i) section 32 of the Small Landholders (Scotland) Act 1911 applies; or (ii) any of the provisions of the Small Landholders (Scotland) Acts 1886 to 1931 applies; and

(b) no part of the holding is leased other than as a tenancy mentioned in (a) above.

Public notification of any such application has to be given by the Crofting Commission. Comments on the application can be submitted to the Crofting Commission and there does not appear to be any restriction on who can submit such comments.

In determining the application, the Crofting Commission shall have regard to (a) such comments, if any, as are duly made to them; (b) the public interest and as the case may be the interests of the crofting community in the locality of the land; and (c) whether social or economic benefits might be expected as a consequence of so constituting it.

If a new croft is constituted by the Crofting Commission then it will require to be registered in the Crofting Register.

Where a new croft has been constituted as a result of an application made by a tenant of a holding the Crofting Commission must not forward the application for registration in the Crofting

Register to the Keeper of the Registers of Scotland unless they are satisfied:-

(a) that agreement has been reached between the applicant and the owner of the land as to an amount to be paid by the applicant to the owner in compensation for the holding being constituted as a croft and that the amount has been duly paid;

(b) that the applicant and the owner have agreed that no amount in compensation is to be so payable; or

(c) that any such amount found, by virtue of the procedure to be outlined in the next paragraph, to be so payable has been duly paid.

If no agreement can be reached between the applicant and the owner then the compensation payable by the applicant to the owner in compensation for the holding being constituted as a croft is to be the difference between (a) the value of the holding assuming that it is not to be so constituted; and (b) its value assuming that it is so constituted, and is to be assessed by a valuer appointed by the applicant and the owner.

Where the applicant and the owner are unable to agree as to such an appointment the valuer is to be appointed by the Scottish Land Court or by a person nominated by the Court.

The valuer must, within six weeks after being appointed, send to the owner and the applicant a notice in writing specifying the compensation payable and setting out how its amount was calculated.

The expenses of the valuer are to be met by the applicant.

The owner or the applicant may appeal to the Lands Tribunal for Scotland against the assessment carried out by the valuer.

It should be noted that if the owner of land applies to create a new croft then they cannot immediately become an owner-occupier crofter, or the crofting tenant, on that land being constituted as a croft. They will instead become the landlord of a vacant croft.

CHAPTER SIXTEEN
CROFTING COMMUNITY RIGHT TO BUY

The 1997 Act enables Scottish Ministers to dispose of a crofting property that they own to an approved body, representative of the crofting interests in that property.

However, there was no rush by crofters on estates owned and managed by the Scottish Government to do so. The first time that this ability to buy was utilised was in 2010 when the West Harris Trust acquired three contiguous estates extending to 16,000 hectares.

Part 3 of the 2003 Act as amended by the 2015 Act and again by the 2016 Act gives crofting communities a right to buy their land whether or not the land is for sale, where the application can be shown to be in the public interest.

A suitable crofting community body will have to be set up for the purpose of purchasing the land. Such a body must either be a company limited by guarantee, a Scottish charitable incorporated organisation or a community benefit society. There are detailed provisions in Part 3 of the 2003 Act as to what the body's articles of association, constitution or registered rules (as the case may be) must include. The body will only be a crofting community body once Scottish Ministers have given it written confirmation that they are satisfied that the main purpose of the body is consistent with furthering the achievement of sustainable development.

The land to be purchased must be "eligible croft land" which means:-

(a) land within the meaning of “croft” given by the 1993 Act together with any land or right which is deemed to be a croft or part thereof (including arable machair and scattalds);

(b) any land in which a tenant of a croft, whether alone or in common with others, has a right of pasture or grazing;

(c) any land:-

(i) comprising any part of a common grazing held by a tenant of a croft; or

(ii) held runrig [in-bye land divided into strips ("rigs") periodically reassigned among the tenants of a township so that no individual has continuous use of the best land] by a tenant of a croft,

which has not been apportioned for the exclusive use of a tenant of a croft under the 1993 Act; and

(d) any land which consists of salmon fishings in inland waters within or contiguous to, or mineral rights (other than rights to oil, coal, gas, gold or silver) in, land referred to in paragraphs (a) to (c) above (including any such fishings or rights which are owned separately from that land).

Eligible croft land does not, however, include any croft occupied or worked by its owner or a member of its owner’s family.

The right is given to purchase interposed leases from the tenants thereunder. This for example would cover a not uncommon situation where a lease is granted by a landowner of a crofting estate to say a wind farm developer often still subject to planning consents and the consent of the Scottish Land Court (Chapter 10) being obtained to the proposed wind farm development actually taking place. This provision does not apply to a tenancy which is either a croft tenancy or the tenancy of a dwelling-house.

Where eligible croft land is being bought eligible additional land and/or eligible sporting interests may also be bought.

"eligible additional land" means:-

(a) any part of which is contiguous to the eligible croft land which is being bought by the body; and

(b) owned by the owner of such eligible croft land,

other than land which consists of salmon fishings in inland waters within or contiguous to, or mineral rights in, such land.

"eligible sporting interests" means the rights of a person other than the owner of eligible croft land under any lease or other contract to shoot or fish on the land but that does not include any right under a lease of salmon fishings in inland waters within or contiguous to eligible croft land.

The application for consent to purchase must be made by the crofting community body to the Scottish Ministers.

The Scottish Ministers shall invite views in writing from those having an interest in the application, including the Crofting Commission, to be received within 60 days. Public notice of the application shall also be given.

The crofting community body will have an opportunity to respond to any views received by Scottish Ministers.

Scottish Ministers shall, when considering whether to consent to an application, have regard to all views on it and responses which they have received.

Scottish Ministers must be satisfied that the crofting community have approved the proposal to exercise the right to buy. This requires a ballot of the members of the crofting community to be held with the majority voting in favour of the proposition that the crofting community body exercises its right to buy.

Where the owner of any eligible additional land to which an application to purchase relates has not requested, or consented to, the sale of that land Scottish Ministers shall refer to the Scottish Land Court the question of whether the eligible additional land may be bought by the crofting community body without the consent of its owner.

A landowner may request that eligible additional land or further eligible additional land be included in any purchase. Scottish Ministers may, if they consider that it is in the public interest to do so, make it a condition of their proceeding to consider the application by the crofting community body that the body modifies its application so as to include in the land to be bought that eligible additional land as further such land.

At any time before Scottish Ministers reach a decision, they or others with an interest may refer to the Scottish Land Court any question (other than a question which Scottish Ministers may, or may be required to, refer under specific provisions in Part 3 of the 2003 Act) relating to the application.

There are provisions to allow the leaseback to the landowner of sporting interests.

Where Scottish Ministers consent to an application to purchase they shall appoint a valuer, being a person who appears to them to be suitably qualified, independent and to have knowledge and experience of valuing land or interests of a kind which is similar to the land, tenant's interest or sporting interests being bought, to assess the value of the land, tenant's interest or sporting interests to which the application relates.

The question of the valuation once determined by the valuer can be appealed to the Scottish Land Court.

The Scottish Ministers' decision on the application can be appealed to the relevant Sheriff Court with jurisdiction for the area that the land in question is situated in.

The Crofting Commission had to set up and keep (or secure that there was set up and kept) a register to be known as the Register of Crofting Community Rights to Buy to record all applications made under Part 3 of the 2003 Act. This register is not available online and you must contact the Crofting Commission by letter or e-mail for information contained in it.

CHAPTER SEVENTEEN
SUCCESSION

There are three distinct parts to crofting succession: (i) making a will to bequeath an interest in a croft; (ii) what happens after death where there is a will (testate succession); and (iii) what happens after death where there is no will (intestacy).

Bequest of a Croft

Whilst an owner-occupied croft can be bequeathed in a will to as many people as you like so that they would all become co-owners of that croft, the position with regard to a tenanted croft is not so simple.

A croft tenancy may only be bequeathed in a will to any one natural person; or to two or more natural persons provided that (i) each person would come into the place of the crofter in relation to the tenancy of part of the croft; and (ii) no part of the croft would, were all the bequests accepted, be untenanted.

This, in effect, means the croft having to be divided into different parts. Any such bequest on this basis is null and void if the Crofting Commission does not give their consent to the division of the croft. If their consent is given but there is a failure to register the division in the Crofting Register that also renders the bequest null and void.

If a crofter does want to divide their croft in this way, as part of a bequest of a crofting tenancy to more than one natural person, then they are probably going to have to include a map in their will showing the proposed division. It would also be wise to provide for the possibility of the Crofting Commission refusing consent and a fall-back position to avoid the bequest becoming null and void and falling into intestacy.

An alternative, of course, is to purchase the tenancy, become an owner-occupier crofter and bequeath the owner-occupied croft to a number of future co-owners.

If a will is wrongly drafted so as not to comply with the provisions of the 1993 Act the bequest is likely to be null and void and fall to be dealt with according to the law of intestacy.

The residency and cultivation obligations should also be borne in mind when deciding who to bequest a croft tenancy to. There may be little point leaving that tenancy to someone who does not reside (and is unlikely to relocate to reside) on or within 32 kilometres of the croft and/or who will have no interest in cultivating the croft.

Testate Succession

Following the death of a crofter who has left a will bequeathing a croft tenancy the legatee (beneficiary) must, if they accept the bequest (a) give notice of the bequest to the landlord, and (b) send a copy of the notice to the Crofting Commission, before the end of a period of 12 months beginning with the death of the crofter. Failure to do so within the 12-month period renders the bequest null and void. It would then have to be dealt with according to the law of intestacy. An executor of the deceased crofter authorised to do so by a legatee may give the notice to the landlord and copy it to the Crofting Commission.

Notwithstanding that a legatee comes into the place of the deceased crofter, the tenancy is an asset of the deceased crofter's estate, available along with the other assets of the estate to meet the other expenses of administration, and debts, of the estate; and any such legatee is liable to contribute to such expenses and debts accordingly.

Intestacy

If there is no will or a bequest in a will is invalid or becomes null and void then the law of intestacy will apply. This may result in a croft tenancy going to someone that the deceased crofter did not want to get it or the croft tenancy having to be sold for the proceeds to be split amongst a number of beneficiaries on intestacy.

If the tenancy is, on intestacy, to be transferred to one natural person then a docquet should be inserted onto a certificate of confirmation narrating the transfer and be signed by the executor. Similar to testate succession, in this instance the executor must (a) give notice of the transfer containing particulars of the transferee to the landlord, who shall accept the transferee as tenant; and (b) at the same time send a copy of the notice to the Crofting Commission.

However, unlike testate succession the period required to give the notice in this instance is 24 months rather than 12 months.

If the requisite notice is not given then the Crofting Commission has the power to give notice that they propose to terminate the tenancy and declare the croft to be vacant.

There then remains the ability for the tenancy to still be transferred albeit after the 24-month period with the ultimate sanction, if that is not happening, of the tenancy being terminated.

Registration

The transfer of a croft either under testate succession or on intestacy will also trigger first registration in the Crofting Register or be an event affecting a registered croft that must be registered in that register.

MORE BOOKS BY LAW BRIEF PUBLISHING

A selection of our other titles available now:-

'A Practical Guide to the SRA Principles, Individual and Law Firm Codes of Conduct 2019 – What Every Law Firm Needs to Know' by Paul Bennett
'A Practical Guide to Licensing Law for Commercial Property Lawyers' by Niall McCann & Richard Williams
'A Practical Guide to Adoption for Family Lawyers' by Graham Pegg
'Essential Motor Finance Law for the Busy Practitioner' by Richard Humphreys
'A Practical Guide to Industrial Disease Claims' by Andrew Mckie & Ian Skeate
'Employment Law and the Gig Economy' by Nigel Mackay & Annie Powell
'A Practical Guide to the Law of Armed Conflict' by Jo Morris & Libby Anderson
'A Practical Guide to Redundancy' by Philip Hyland
'A Practical Guide to Vicarious Liability' by Mariel Irvine
'A Practical Guide to Claims Arising from Delays in Diagnosing Cancer' by Bella Webb
'A Practical Guide to Applications for Landlord's Consent and Variation of Leases' by Mark Shelton
'A Practical Guide to Relief from Sanctions Post-Mitchell and Denton' by Peter Causton
'Butler's Equine Tax Planning: 2nd Edition' by Julie Butler
'A Practical Guide to Equity Release for Advisors' by Paul Sams
'A Practical Guide to Immigration Law and Tier 1 Entrepreneur Applications' by Sarah Pinder
'A Practical Guide to Unlawful Eviction and Harassment' by Stephanie Lovegrove
'In My Backyard! A Practical Guide to Neighbourhood Plans' by Dr Sue Chadwick
'A Practical Guide to the Law Relating to Food' by Ian Thomas

'A Practical Guide to the Ending of Assured Shorthold Tenancies' by Elizabeth Dwomoh
'Commercial Mediation – A Practical Guide' by Nick Carr
'A Practical Guide to Financial Services Claims' by Chris Hegarty
'The Law of Houses in Multiple Occupation: A Practical Guide to HMO Proceedings' by Julian Hunt
'A Practical Guide to Unlawful Eviction and Harassment' by Stephanie Lovegrove
'A Practical Guide to Solicitor and Client Costs' by Robin Dunne
'Artificial Intelligence – The Practical Legal Issues' by John Buyers
'A Practical Guide to Wrongful Conception, Wrongful Birth and Wrongful Life Claims' by Rebecca Greenstreet
'Occupiers, Highways and Defective Premises Claims: A Practical Guide Post-Jackson – 2nd Edition' by Andrew Mckie
'A Practical Guide to Financial Ombudsman Service Claims' by Adam Temple & Robert Scrivenor
'A Practical Guide to the Law of Enfranchisement and Lease Extension' by Paul Sams
'A Practical Guide to Marketing for Lawyers – 2nd Edition' by Catherine Bailey & Jennet Ingram
'A Practical Guide to Advising Schools on Employment Law' by Jonathan Holden
'Certificates of Lawful Use and Development: A Guide to Making and Determining Applications' by Bob Mc Geady & Meyric Lewis
'A Practical Guide to the Law of Dilapidations' by Mark Shelton
'A Practical Guide to the 2018 Jackson Personal Injury and Costs Reforms' by Andrew Mckie
'A Guide to Consent in Clinical Negligence Post-Montgomery' by Lauren Sutherland QC
'A Practical Guide to Running Housing Disrepair and Cavity Wall Claims: 2nd Edition' by Andrew Mckie & Ian Skeate
'A Practical Guide to the General Data Protection Regulation (GDPR)' by Keith Markham
'A Practical Guide to Digital and Social Media Law for Lawyers' by Sherree Westell

'A Practical Guide to Holiday Sickness Claims – 2nd Edition' by Andrew Mckie & Ian Skeate
'A Practical Guide to Inheritance Act Claims by Adult Children Post-Ilott v Blue Cross' by Sheila Hamilton Macdonald
'A Practical Guide to Elderly Law' by Justin Patten
'Arguments and Tactics for Personal Injury and Clinical Negligence Claims' by Dorian Williams
'A Practical Guide to QOCS and Fundamental Dishonesty' by James Bentley
'A Practical Guide to Drone Law' by Rufus Ballaster, Andrew Firman, Eleanor Clot
'Practical Mediation: A Guide for Mediators, Advocates, Advisers, Lawyers, and Students in Civil, Commercial, Business, Property, Workplace, and Employment Cases' by Jonathan Dingle with John Sephton
'Practical Horse Law: A Guide for Owners and Riders' by Brenda Gilligan
'A Comparative Guide to Standard Form Construction and Engineering Contracts' by Jon Close
'A Practical Guide to Compliance for Personal Injury Firms Working With Claims Management Companies' by Paul Bennett
'A Practical Guide to the Landlord and Tenant Act 1954: Commercial Tenancies' by Richard Hayes & David Sawtell
'A Practical Guide to Personal Injury Claims Involving Animals' by Jonathan Hand
'A Practical Guide to Psychiatric Claims in Personal Injury' by Liam Ryan
'Introduction to the Law of Community Care in England and Wales' by Alan Robinson
'A Practical Guide to Dog Law for Owners and Others' by Andrea Pitt
'Ellis and Kevan on Credit Hire – 5th Edition' by Aidan Ellis & Tim Kevan
'RTA Allegations of Fraud in a Post-Jackson Era: The Handbook – 2nd Edition' by Andrew Mckie
'RTA Personal Injury Claims: A Practical Guide Post-Jackson' by Andrew Mckie
'On Experts: CPR35 for Lawyers and Experts' by David Boyle
'An Introduction to Personal Injury Law' by David Boyle
'A Practical Guide to Claims Arising From Accidents Abroad and Travel Claims' by Andrew Mckie & Ian Skeate

'A Practical Guide to Cosmetic Surgery Claims' by Dr Victoria Handley
'A Practical Guide to Chronic Pain Claims' by Pankaj Madan
'A Practical Guide to Claims Arising from Fatal Accidents' by James Patience
'A Practical Approach to Clinical Negligence Post-Jackson' by Geoffrey Simpson-Scott
'A Practical Guide to Personal Injury Trusts' by Alan Robinson
'Employers' Liability Claims: A Practical Guide Post-Jackson' by Andrew Mckie
'A Practical Guide to Subtle Brain Injury Claims' by Pankaj Madan
'The Law of Driverless Cars: An Introduction' by Alex Glassbrook
'A Practical Guide to Costs in Personal Injury Cases' by Matthew Hoe
'A Practical Guide to Alternative Dispute Resolution in Personal Injury Claims – Getting the Most Out of ADR Post-Jackson' by Peter Causton, Nichola Evans, James Arrowsmith
'A Practical Guide to Personal Injuries in Sport' by Adam Walker & Patricia Leonard
'The No Nonsense Solicitors' Practice: A Guide To Running Your Firm' by Bettina Brueggemann
'Baby Steps: A Guide to Maternity Leave and Maternity Pay' by Leah Waller
'The Queen's Counsel Lawyer's Omnibus: 20 Years of Cartoons from The Times 1993-2013' by Alex Steuart Williams

These books and more are available to order online direct from the publisher at www.lawbriefpublishing.com, where you can also read free sample chapters. For any queries, contact us on 0844 587 2383 or mail@lawbriefpublishing.com.

Our books are also usually in stock at www.amazon.co.uk with free next day delivery for Prime members, and at good legal bookshops such as Wildy & Sons.

We are regularly launching new books in our series of practical day-to-day practitioners' guides. Visit our website and join our free newsletter to be kept informed and to receive special offers, free chapters, etc.

You can also follow us on Twitter at www.twitter.com/lawbriefpub.

www.ingramcontent.com/pod-product-compliance
Lightning Source LLC
LaVergne TN
LVHW022304200926
848481LV00004B/1213
* 9 7 8 1 9 1 2 6 8 7 3 9 8 *